Elephants
at Work

Julia Barnes

GARETH**STEVENS**, INC.

A Member of the WRC Media Family of Companies

Please visit our Web site at: www.garethstevens.com
For a free color catalog describing Gareth Stevens Publishing's list of high-quality books and multimedia programs, call 1-800-542-2595 (USA) or 1-800-387-3178 (Canada). Gareth Stevens Publishing's fax: (414) 332-3567.

Library of Congress Cataloging-in-Publication Data

Barnes, Julia.
    Elephants at work / Julia Barnes.— North American ed.
       p. cm. — (Animals at work)
    Includes bibliographical references and index.
    ISBN 0-8368-6224-4 (lib. bdg.)
    1. Working elephants—Juvenile literature. I. Title.
    SF401.E3B37 2006
    636.9'67—dc22   2005054067

This North American edition first published in 2006 by
Gareth Stevens Publishing
A WRC Media Company
330 West Olive Street, Suite 100
Milwaukee, WI 53212 USA

This U.S. edition copyright © 2006 by Gareth Stevens, Inc. Original edition copyright © 2005 by Westline Publishing, The Warren, Aylburton, Lydney, Gloucestershire, GL15 6DX.

Gareth Stevens editor: Carol Ryback
Gareth Stevens designer: Charlie Dahl

Photo Credits:
Bob Davies Photography: 6, 7, 29.
Top Draw: 14, 23, 24, 25, 26, 27.
All other photographs: Jay International.

Printed in the United States of America

1 2 3 4 5 6 7 8 9 10 09 08 07 06

Contents

Introduction

Elephants are the largest land animals. For centuries, humans have often employed brutal methods to tame these mighty creatures and turn them into working animals.

Military commanders used elephants to transport supplies and troops across vast distances and a variety of landscapes. Farmers still harness the colossal strength of elephants to tear down forests and clear cropland. Elephants also play a special role in religious festivals and social traditions in many modern societies.

Discover:
- How elephants are trained
- How many commands an elephant can learn
- Who cares for working elephants
- The dangers involved in working with elephants
- Elephants as circus performers

In *Elephants At Work*, we enter the world of working elephants and learn how humans tame and train them. We will also discover what is involved in their care and what the future holds for working and wild elephants.

Humans and elephants have worked together for centuries.

Where Do Elephants Live?

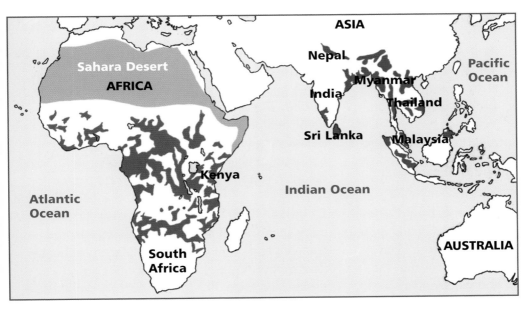

■ = areas populated by African elephants

■ = areas populated by Asian elephants

Africa has about 600,000 elephants in the wild. Their numbers have fallen dramatically, mostly due to a big increase in the **illegal** trade in ivory (see page 29). The number of elephants in Kenya fell from 167,000 in 1970 to 60,000 by 1980 — and to only about 22,000 by 1989. Surveys show that more than half of Africa's elephants were lost to ivory poaching in a ten-year period.

About 50,000 Asian elephants live in the wild. Their numbers have dropped because of forest clearance, farming, and development. Areas where elephants can roam wild are limited.

Approximately 15,000 working elephants are kept in Nepal, India, Sri Lanka, Myanmar (formerly Burma), Malaysia, and Thailand.

Getting To Know Elephants

Gentle giants who roamed the world

Why should an elephant, more than twenty times bigger than a person, work for humans? The elephants simply have no choice in the matter. For centuries, humans have taken young elephants from the wild (see page 17) and tamed them to work. This often meant that the mother elephant was killed. Young elephants separated from their family groups learned to obey humans. Elephants proved to be outstanding helpers and continue to fulfill many different roles.

Origins

Early ancestors of the elephant appeared on Earth about fifty-eight million years ago. As time went on, elephants became bigger and stronger, and by the Pleistocene Era — about two million years ago — elephant ancestors lived all over the world except for Australia, New Zealand, and Antarctica. Elephant ancestors adapted easily to different **habitats** — from hot deserts to cold mountain climates.

Male and female African elephants have tusks.

DID YOU KNOW
Hunting elephants for their ivory tusks is illegal. Unfortunately, *poachers* still kill thousands of elephants annually.

An Asian elephant has smaller ears than an African elephant.

African and Asian elephants

Today, elephants are found naturally in only Africa and Southeast Asia. The two types of elephants are easy to tell apart.

- Size: African elephants are bigger. They weigh up to 7 tons (6.4 tonnes) and measure 10 to 13 feet (3 to 4 meters) high at the shoulder. In contrast, an Asian elephant seldom weighs more than 5 tons (4.5 tonnes), and stands about 7 to 11 feet (2 to 3.5 m) high.

- Ears: African elephants have extremely large ears (*see page 6*).
- Tusks: Male (bull) and female (cow) African elephants both have tusks. Only the Asian bull elephant has tusks (*see page 29*).
- Trunk: An African elephant has two lips at the end of its trunk. An Asian elephant has only one lip (*see page 29*).

Working elephants

Asian elephants are traditionally used for work. The Asian elephant is smaller and easier to handle than an African elephant. Also, the type of work an elephant can do is better suited to the conditions found in Southeast Asia.

Both African and Asian elephants are intelligent animals. They have one of the biggest brains in the animal kingdom. An adult elephant's brain can weigh nearly 11 pounds (5 kilograms).

War Elephants

Going into battle two thousand years ago

Elephants served in an army more than two thousand years ago! Army elephants served a dual purpose: Soldiers rode them into battle, and their tremendous strength ferried soldiers and supplies across the battlefields.

Elephant charge

In battle, elephants were used to trample the enemy. Only male elephants served in the army. Bull elephants are faster and more **aggressive**. A charging elephant can reach a speed of 25 miles (40 kilometers) per hour. These charging giants spread panic and terror through the enemy lines.

Hannibal's army

One of the most famous accounts of war elephants dates back to 218 B.C., when General Hannibal of Carthage crossed the Alps to invade Italy. Hannibal had thirty-eight trained African elephants when he set out on a six-month trek with his army — which included twenty thousand foot soldiers as well as six thousand mounted, or **cavalry**, troops.

The army endured terrible conditions. As if the freezing cold temperatures weren't enough, the elephants and troops had to travel

When charging, a bull elephant like this one is a frightening sight.

Army life was often tough on elephants. Many lost their lives in battle or during transit.

over steep, icy mountain slopes. Native hill tribes also attacked Hannibal's troops, and at least one landslide blocked their progress. Only a few of the elephants made it across the Alps and into Italy.

The Indian army

India used elephants for front-line fighting in wars until the early nineteenth century. During that time, a staggering number were killed. After the invention of the musket (a type of gun) in the seventeenth century, fewer elephants were

used in battle — but that did not signal the end of the elephants' role in war. Elephants could travel long distances over rough **terrain**, carrying huge burdens. They remained an essential part of the supply chain because they transported food, soldiers, weapons, **ammunition**, tents, and other supplies.

Last stand

Elephants were last recruited for war during World War II (1939–1945) when they transported troops and supplies on the border between India and

Burma (now Myanmar). The huge beasts could reach areas where no vehicles could go. They were also used for road and bridge construction in remote areas. Elephants transported building materials to a construction site, cleared the site, and then helped with the construction by carrying supplies to where they were needed.

> ### DID YOU KNOW
> **In Germany during World War II, Hitler was so desperate to save gasoline that instead of using tractors, he commandeered elephants from the Hamburg Zoo to plow the land.**

Sacred Elephants

A special place in certain religions

While the elephant is highly valued as a working animal, it holds an even greater significance in its Asian homeland. Religions in India and Sri Lanka consider elephants holy animals.

Religious links

The elephant played such an important role in the daily routine that it soon became part of the local religious life. Elephants are worshipped by both **Hindus** and **Buddhists**.

The Hindu god Lord Ganesha has the head of an elephant and the body of a human. Some Hindus believe that parts of an elephant's body represent various gods, as shown below.

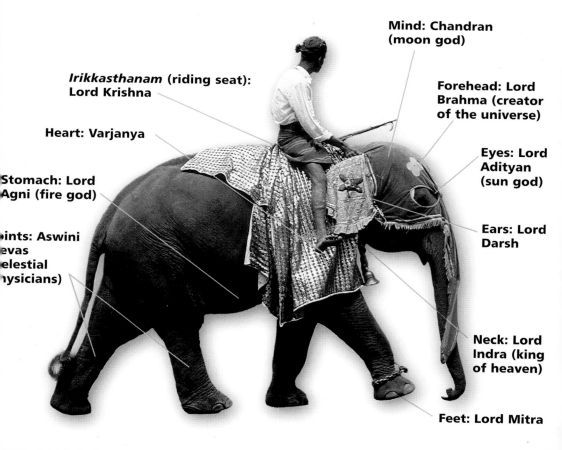

Mind: Chandran (moon god)

Irikkasthanam (riding seat): **Lord Krishna**

Forehead: Lord Brahma (creator of the universe)

Heart: Varjanya

Eyes: Lord Adityan (sun god)

Stomach: Lord Agni (fire god)

Ears: Lord Darsh

ints: Aswini evas elestial hysicians)

Neck: Lord Indra (king of heaven)

Feet: Lord Mitra

Elephants play an important part in religious festivals.

Elephants are also connected to the Buddhist religion. Believers say that an elephant nudged Lord Buddha's mother. By 231 B.C., the elephant had become the **emblem** of Buddhism.

Elephant festivals

Religious festivals are as important in India and Sri Lanka today as they were in ancient times. Ceremonies have remained unchanged for hundreds of years, and the elephant — dressed in elaborate costume — is the most honored figure in processions to and from the temples.

One of the most spectacular festivals is the *Perahera*, which has been staged every year since A.D. 300. The *Perahera* is a ten-day pageant, staged in July or August, that takes place in Kandy, Sri Lanka. One hundred elephants, ridden by their **mahouts**, parade in spectacular nighttime processions. The streets are lined with **pilgrims** who come

to see the traditional dancers, musicians, fire-juggling acrobats, and torch bearers.

The festival, which asks for the blessing of rain for a successful harvest, combines Hindu and Buddhist beliefs. Elephants are "the clouds who walk the Earth" — responsible for bringing vital rain at harvesttime.

The chief elephant that heads the parade bears a tooth belonging to Lord Buddha. This position is considered a great honor, and the elephant that carries the tooth is always a tusker — a bull elephant with tusks.

Preparing for a parade

Handling an elephant in an *ezhunnallippu* —

a festival parade — requires practice and extreme care. Elephants are specially selected and trained from an early age. When they are not being used for religious ceremonies, these elephants return to their work in the forests (see *page 14*).

The mahout must ensure that his elephant stands still while the

Left: The *Perahera* is the most spectacular of all the elephant festivals.

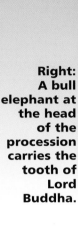

Right: A bull elephant at the head of the procession carries the tooth of Lord Buddha.

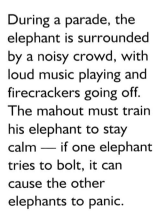

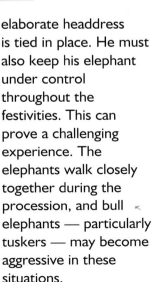

elaborate headdress is tied in place. He must also keep his elephant under control throughout the festivities. This can prove a challenging experience. The elephants walk closely together during the procession, and bull elephants — particularly tuskers — may become aggressive in these situations.

During a parade, the elephant is surrounded by a noisy crowd, with loud music playing and firecrackers going off. The mahout must train his elephant to stay calm — if one elephant tries to bolt, it can cause the other elephants to panic.

There is one further danger that the mahouts must watch

for: The elephant may be required to stand still for long periods during the ceremonies, and some may even fall asleep on their feet. The mahout must awaken the elephant gently, patting it on the back, or talking loudly. If the elephant is awakened too suddenly, it may sometimes attack the mahout.

Harnessing Power

Carrying loads and clearing forests

The history of the elephant as a working animal in Southeast Asia goes back four thousand years. Ancient records describe how tame elephants were, and how easily elephants were brought in from the wild and trained.

Beasts of burden

Nepal, India, Sri Lanka, Malaysia, Thailand, and Myanmar (see page 5), still use elephants to transport timber, minerals (such as tin), and farm produce. Elephants are also used on **construction sites** for roads, railroads, and bridges.

In the forests

When working in dense forest, the elephant is especially impressive. It combines its great intelligence with its incredible strength. Elephants are trained to perform the following tasks:

- Clearing areas of forest for use as farmland or for building houses.
- Dragging logs.
- Stacking logs in a pile.
- Moving logs forward or backward using their feet.
- Pushing logs forward using their head.
- Loading logs onto a truck.

The mighty elephant is able to carry heavy loads. It can transport people and supplies.

DID YOU KNOW

Just as people are right-handed or left-handed, elephants often use one tusk more than the other.

The mahout works with his elephant to move a pile of logs.

- Using their trunk and tusks to carry smaller logs to other areas.

Soft spot
The elephant has a soft spot at the back of each ear. The mahout uses his bare feet on these sensitive areas to steer and give commands (see page 17).

Brain power
There is probably a lot of truth to the saying "An elephant never forgets." Elephant brains need to store a lot of information.

To survive in the wild, an elephant must be able to:

- recognize different elephants in the herd.
- remember the behavior of each elephant in the herd.
- recall the good feeding sites.
- store experiences of coping and living through difficult times, such as finding enough water during droughts.
- establish a memory bank of dangerous places and situations.

The elephant's ability to learn — and to remember — makes it a highly prized working animal.

> ### DID YOU KNOW
> Scientists believe that elephants are intelligent enough to understand how other elephants are feeling, such as when they mourn.

A Special Relationship

The bond between mahout and elephant

The elephant is trained and cared for by a mahout, or elephant trainer. The mahout must have a thorough knowledge of elephant behavior, for he can be exposed to great dangers. An elephant will obey orders dutifully — but this can change in a split second if the elephant becomes angry or feels it is being mistreated.

Training mahouts

There is no formal system for training mahouts. In many cases, it is a family tradition, sometimes going back hundreds of years, in which a father teaches

A mahout works with an elephant when it is first taken from the wild. He gradually tames it.

DID YOU KNOW
In Myanmar, mahouts are called *oozies*; in Thailand, they are called *kao-chang*.

Over a period of time, the elephant learns to be obedient and follow the mahout's commands.

his son, passing down his skill and knowledge. A young boy will be matched with a young elephant, and the two will grow up together. When they are both old enough, they will start full-time work. This is often the beginning of a lifelong bond.

The trainee mahout must learn:

- how to care for an elephant. It is the responsibility of the mahout to keep his elephant fit and healthy.
- the commands and signals for working with an elephant. An elephant may learn up to fifteen verbal commands and as many hand, foot, or toe signals.
- to understand elephant behavior, so he can spot early

signs of trouble (*see page 19*).
- how to get the elephant to accept him as its boss or leader — so the elephant will be obedient.

Taming elephants

Elephants have always been taken from the wild and trained, so every elephant presents a challenge to the mahout. In most cases, an elephant will be caught when it is about three years old. It will gradually learn to accept being handled by people.

The elephant must understand that it is no longer a wild animal that can go anywhere it chooses. It has to get used to being held by heavy chains, which restrict its freedom. In most cases, the mahout

attaches a chain to a hind leg. The chain is secured to a tree or a strong post. Sometimes, a body chain that goes around the elephant's body and is tied to a hind leg is used. This chain gives the mahout maximum control, which he needs in the early stages of training.

When he is riding, the mahout attaches a double rope around the elephant's neck. The mahout puts his feet through the rope, which keeps his feet in the correct position to give toe commands.

Tools of the Trade

How to train an elephant to work

When training an animal as big as an elephant, there are only a few training aids that help. Most mahouts use:

- a short-handled iron hook, or **ankus**. The elephant learns to pull toward or push away from the point of the mahout's ankus.

- a wooden rod, approximately ten feet (3 m) long. The rod helps train the elephant to stand in one place. It learns not to push the rod down. The rod can also be used to prod the elephant from a distance.
- a knife, for cutting down branches, grass, and other food for the elephant. This is also the mahout's sole weapon if the elephant attacks.

A special hook, called an ankus, is used for controlling which way an elephant moves.

The mahout makes sure the elephant is in a good mood before he asks it to work.

Approaching an elephant

Over a period of time, a mahout and his elephant will develop a special relationship where they trust each other, and the elephant accepts the mahout as boss. But the mahout must always be respectful, keeping a close watch on the elephant's behavior. When a mahout approaches his elephant, he must always go through the following **ritual** to ensure that his elephant will cooperate:

• The mahout must be calm and approach the elephant quietly.

• The mahout will usually say a prayer to his favorite god before mounting the elephant.

• The elephant is always approached from the left side. The mahout commands the elephant to move to the right.

• An elephant in a cooperative mood will beat its trunk on the ground, **urinate**, and **defecate**. This is a sign of **submission**, showing that the elephant accepts the mahout as boss.

• If the elephant is reluctant to work, it will sniff the mahout with its trunk, shake its head, or rub its body against a tree. These are signs of protest.

• If the mahout sees signs of protest, he will command the elephant to lie down. The elephant knows it must obey that command before its mahout will release the chains that are restraining it.

Danger Time

Dealing with bull elephants

Female elephants are generally easier to train than males. They are more willing to accept the mahout as a leader, and they are less likely to pick fights with other elephants.

After his bull elephant is fully grown, or mature, the mahout must be especially careful with his animal. After about age twenty, a bull elephant comes into "**musth**" annually. *Musth* is a Hindi word meaning drunk or intoxicated. It clearly describes a male elephant's behavior at this time.

Bull elephants come into musth at the same time that female (cow) elephants are ready for breeding. For up to sixty days, the bull elephant will want to do nothing but find females ready for mating, and will compete with other males. He will almost stop eating, and he will be moody and aggressive.

An elephant in musth is a dangerous animal.

An elephant in musth will not work, and the mahout must keep his distance.

Handling an elephant in musth

The early signs of an elephant coming into musth include:

- frequent sniffing of the mahout and other people with its trunk.
- swift changes of mood and behavior.
- a fixed gaze — the elephant stares at an object for a long time.
- saliva dribbling from the trunk.
- urine dribbling constantly.

- swollen **temporal glands**. A gland on each side of the head between the eyes and the ears swells up during musth.
- eyes that appear bright and red.

During musth, a mahout will not work his elephant. It is risky even to go near an elephant in musth — many mahouts have been killed by their elephants at this time.

An elephant in musth will be restrained with special, heavy chains. A front leg and a hind leg are tied. Except for providing food and water, the mahout will leave his elephant alone.

Many mahouts believe that, with careful attention to an elephant during the first musth, the animal will be easier to handle and less aggressive the next time it comes into musth.

Work, Rest, and Play

Providing for the needs of a working elephant

A mahout and his elephant share their lives completely, spending almost all their time together. The mahout works long hours with his elephant. He must also make sure that his elephant has a place to rest and enough food to eat.

Finding food

An elephant eats about 400 pounds (180 kg) of food daily. The mahout must provide the right diet to meet the needs of a working elephant.

In some camps, elephants are allowed to graze in the forest overnight. The mahout attaches a long chain, called a trailing chain, to the elephant's hind leg and ties a bell around the elephant's neck so he can find his animal in the morning.

In many cases, the mahout harvests food for his elephant. Equipped with his knife, the mahout climbs date and coconut trees and cuts branches to bring back to the elephant. Climbing the trees with the sharp knife and cutting the branches often proves extremely dangerous for mahouts.

In addition, the working elephant receives a daily helping of grains, beans, and lentils to add protein and other nutrient to its diet.

Elephants sometimes rub against trees to scratch their itches.

Elephants consider bath time the high point of their day.

Resting place

When an elephant is not working, its mahout will **tether** it in a shady area with access to fresh drinking water. An elephant drinks between 30 and 50 gallons (114 to 190 liters) of water a day. The mahout may need to carry the water from a nearby stream. Ideally, an elephant's resting area should be fairly soft and muddy. The mahout should keep it free from droppings.

Bath time

The highlight of the working elephant's day is its bath time. In the wild, elephants love to wallow in the mud. They **instinctively** bathe in a river, lake, or stream to keep their skin healthy. Mahouts bathe their elephants for the following reasons:

- It keeps the skin clean.
- It lowers the elephant's body temperature.
- It allows treatment of any minor injuries or wounds.
- Elephants find bathing very relaxing.
- Bath time cements the bond between elephant and mahout.

The mahout teaches his elephant to lie first on one side, then to sit up so its head and neck can be washed. After its legs and feet are attended to, the elephant must lie down on its other side.

Two mahouts will share the job of scrubbing the elephant. It can be dangerous trying to control an elephant in water. The mahouts use a **pumice stone** or a coconut husk for scrubbing the animal's entire body, which is often a lengthy and exhausting process. An elephant bath lasts up to two hours.

Career Change

Challenging times for working elephants

Elephants are still an important part of the timber business in a number of countries in Southeast Asia. Myanmar (formerly Burma) has about five thousand working elephants. Elephants are still widely used in the rough terrain of northwest India. The **traditional role** of the working elephant is threatened, however.

Times of change

Elephants are invaluable for land clearing and logging in remote areas. But what happens when the land has been cleared and no trees are left?

Simply put, the working elephants and their mahouts lose their jobs. In Thailand, only a fraction of the rain forest remains, and in order to save the remaining forest areas, the government banned all logging. In 2000, the mahouts, desperate for work, went into Bangkok, Thailand's capital city, with their elephants and began protesting.

Since then, a number of steps have been taken to find new work for the elephants and their mahouts.

On patrol

In order to protect the small areas of forest that remain, the elephants were recruited for **patrol** duties. Although Thailand banned logging, illegal logging still occurs. Elephants and mahouts on patrol in the forested areas helps prevent illegal logging and keeps mahouts employed.

Training camps have been set up in Thailand so that tourists can see elephants at work.

Most of the trained elephants in Thailand now work in the tourist industry. Visitors can view the animals from close range.

Tourist attraction

Even though the traditional role of the elephant is dying out in Thailand and elsewhere, elephants still play an important role in a country's economy. Tourists love to see elephants at work, and a number of elephant camps have been set up especially for tourists. Visitors watch elephants at work and while they are being bathed by their mahouts. Some elephants are also trained to give rides to tourists and to perform in shows (see *page 26*).

Elephant artists

A few specially selected elephants are also raising money by producing paintings to help support Thailand's mahouts and elephants.

Elephants have long been known to make patterns on the ground with stone and sticks. In the last few decades, elephants in some zoos in the United States were given paints and paintbrushes — and the results were spectacular.

Paintings by elephants are now in big demand. An art team was sent to Thailand to retrain seven elephants left idle by the logging ban for new careers as artists. Elephants do not see colors as well as humans, so the paint colors are chosen for the elephants, but the elephants choose which paint buckets to use for their projects.

A worldwide auction of fifty examples of elephant art from Thailand raised more than $30,000 in 2000. Since then, tourists to Thailand often visit the painting camps and eagerly purchase the elephant artwork.

> **DID YOU KNOW**
> **Ruby, an elephant at the Phoenix Zoo in Arizona, raises $100,000 a year from the sale of her paintings.**

Elephant Entertainers

Tricks and treats make a spectacular show

Performing elephants always attract big crowds.

In the first half of the twentieth century, no circus was complete without its troupe of elephants. People came from all over to marvel at the tricks the massive animals performed.

Elephant trainers use the ancient wisdom of the mahouts when they teach elephants to perform in the circus. Just as mahouts do, the circus trainers work to establish a bond between human and elephant. Many trainers also use food, such as something sweet, or a piece of bread, as a reward.

In the past, trainers made elephants perform tricks — such as balancing on stools, standing on their hind legs, or even doing a

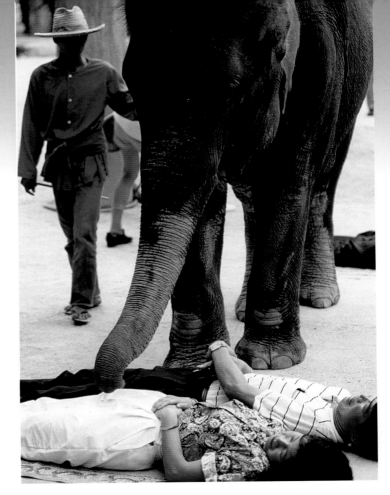

handstand — that were difficult or uncomfortable. Training methods were often harsh, and the animals were kept in cramped conditions.

Today, we have a greater understanding of and compassion for the needs of elephants, and they are treated much better. In most cases now, the tricks elephants perform are based on natural behavior, such as gripping objects with their trunks or walking in processions.

A number of circuses throughout the world still include performing elephants. In Southeast Asia, elephant shows have become a big tourist attraction.

Elephants in zoos

When zoos were first established in the second half of the nineteenth century, no one considered it cruel to keep large animals in cages, and elephants were often confined in enclosures that were far too small for them.

Sometimes a single elephant kept by a zoo was also trained to give rides to visitors.

Zoos have changed dramatically since those early days. Elephants kept in modern zoos enjoy spacious living quarters. They are often part of a breeding family group.

Elephant Fact File

Bulls: Male elephants leave the family group when they are six or seven years old. They live in loose groups with other males, but when they are ready for breeding — at about twenty years of age — they seek out their own living territory.

Ears: Elephant's ears have a special network of blood vessels that act like a natural air-conditioning system — the bigger the ears, the more effective the cooling system.

Over time, African elephants developed bigger ears than Asian elephants to cope with their extremely hot environment.

Hearing: Elephants have excellent hearing — much better than that of humans.

Eyesight: Elephants have small eyes and poor eyesight. They can only see clearly for about 30 to 40 feet (9 to 12 m).

Family groups: In the wild, elephants live in herds or family groups, which generally include an elderly female (cow), two or three of her daughters, and their young offspring. Two or three related families may travel together in "kinship groups."

Food: Elephants are **herbivores**, eating a wide variety of different plants, grasses, and leaves. Asian elephants may eat as many as one hundred different kinds of plants.

In Africa, elephants eat **savanna** grasses. They also forage for roots and eat the bark of trees. In the wild, elephants spend about twenty hours of every day eating.

Gestation: An elephant's pregnancy is exceptionally long, lasting twenty-two months. A newborn baby elephant weighs about 265 lbs. (120 kg).

Habitat: In the wild, elephants roam over large areas, moving on when they need to find food. Forest clearance, land development, and farming have decreased the natural habitats of wild elephants in Africa and Asia.

Life expectancy: Wild elephants can live sixty or more years — but this is increasingly rare because of the threat posed by poachers and loss of habitat.

In the wild, elephants live in close-knit family groups.

Size: Elephants reach their adult size at fifteen years, but they continue to grow throughout their lives. Males grow more quickly than females (*see page 6*).

Skin: An elephant's skin is about one inch (2.54 centimeters) thick, and it has no sweat glands.

Sound: Elephants make a variety of trumpeting sounds. They also make sounds below the range of human hearing. This is known as **infrasound** and can be heard by other elephants several miles (km) away.

Speed: An elephant walks at a speed of between 2 to 3 miles (3 to 5 km) per hour. A charging elephant can run 25 miles (40 km) per hour — much faster than a human.

Trunk: An elephant's nose and upper lip are joined together as its trunk. The trunk has forty thousand muscles but no bones. It allows elephants to feed from trees or the ground, and to break off branches. Elephants also lift things, drink, squirt water, throw dust, greet, or threaten with their trunks.

Tusks: An elephant's overgrown teeth, or tusks, from its upper jaws grow throughout life. Tusks are made of ivory — called "white gold" by poachers because of the high prices ivory brings in illegal markets. Ivory is a good material for carving. It was traditionally made into ornaments and jewelry.

Glossary

aggressive: angry or violent.

ammunition: supplies for weapons, such as bullets for guns.

ankus: a iron hook used to control an elephant.

Buddhists: people who follow a religion based on the teachings of Gautama Buddha.

cavalry: soldiers on horseback.

construction site: a building site.

defecate: to eliminate feces (solid wastes) from the body.

emblem: symbol.

forage: to search for food.

habitats: different environments, such as a forest or a desert.

herbivores: animals that eat plants.

Hindus: people who follow the Hindu religion, possibly the oldest in the world.

illegal: against the law.

infrasound: sounds that are too low in pitch for humans to hear.

instinctively: naturally.

mahouts: elephant trainers.

musth: the time of year when a bull elephant looks for female elephants that are ready to breed.

patrol: a regular tour of an area to guard it or to maintain order.

pilgrims: people who journey to sacred places.

poachers: people who hunt illegally.

pumice stone: a lightweight rock used for scrubbing.

ritual: a ceremonial routine.

savanna: a semitropical grassland.

submission: the adoption of obedience behaviors or routines not naturally practiced.

temporal glands: glands between an elephant's eyes and ears.

terrain: the type of landscape.

tether: a restraint, or tie.

traditional role: the types of jobs for which elephants were first used.

urinate: to eliminate urine (liquid wastes) from the body.

Find Out More . . .

More books to read

Crossingham, John. *What Is An Elephant?* Crabtree (2002).

Darling, Kathy. *The Elephant Hospital.* Millbrook Press (2002).

Holmes, Kevin. *Elephants.* Bridgestone Books (2000).

Redmond, Ian. *Elephant. Eyewitness Books* (series). DK (2000).

Whitehouse, Patricia. *Elephant.* Heinemann (2003).

Web sites

www.awf.org/wildlives/71
Visit the African Wildlife Foundation's Web site.

www.elephant.tnet.co.th/index_29.1.html
Get interesting facts and information on Asian elephants.

www.enchantedlearning.com/subjects/mammals/elephants
Compare the differences between African and Asian elephants.

www.nationalgeographic.com/kids/creature–feature/0103/elephants2.html
Discover more about an elephant's trunk and learn how elephants interact
with each other.

www.pbs.org/wnet/nature/elephants/
Find out about the poaching problem affecting African elephants
and explore links to other elephant information.

Index